CW00954458

THE LIFE OF
SAINT FRANCIS

For Chloe Margaret Francis
with love
R.B.

To Mari and Gina
with love
J.M.

British Library Cataloguing in Publication Data
A catalogue record of this book is available from the British Library

ISBN 0 340 71334 8 (HB)
ISBN 0 340 71427 1 (PB)

First UK edition published in 1999
by Hodder Children's Books,
a division of Hodder Headline plc,
338 Euston Road, London NW1 3BH

10 9 8 7 6 5 4 3 2 1

Printed in Hong Kong

THE LIFE OF
SAINT
FRANCIS

Retold by
RACHEL BILLINGTON

Illustrated by
JAMES MAYHEW

*Hodder
Children's
Books*

A division of Hodder Headline plc

THE LIFE OF SAINT FRANCIS

THE TOWN, CURLED UP LIKE A CAT on the lower slopes of a dark mountain, seemed pale in the morning sun. A swallow flying out from the trees swooped over the curving walls which protected the town against enemies. As the sun reached its highest point, in a sky that was as blue and wide as the sea, the sound of bells, deep, soft, fast, slow, broke into the bright air. The swallow slipped into a hole in a stone turret and disappeared.

Close up, the town was not pale at all but a collection of light and shade. Alleyways trailed like dark ribbons through the houses, suddenly breaking out into the brilliance of squares which spread out like aprons in front of fine churches with their arched doorways, decorated by figures of the saints.

On the edge of town, beside a large church, a heavy oak door burst open and a joyous charge of boys dashed out into the sunshine. They were led by a slight figure, dressed in such colourful clothes that he seemed to flash across the square like a bright plumaged bird.

'Francis! Wait for us!' the boys called and Francis did pause for a moment but only to give him breath to begin a song. His voice, high and clear, rose above the yells of his friends. Although this was an Italian town, he sang in French because that was the language of the troubadours who sang of romance and adventure in distant places. Besides, this boy's name, Francis, meant 'The Frenchman' for his mother had been born in France.

Singing, Francis led his friends through the city, as if they were knights on a crusade to free the Holy Land from wicked infidels. Since early morning the boys had been confined in the cool, semi-darkness of the schoolroom attached to the church of Saint Georgio. They had repeated Latin verbs over and over again under the stern eyes of the priest who taught them.

Now, at last, they were free to march round the ramparts of the city and shake their fists at the rival city of Perugia, which they could just see on the next hill. Descending by crumbling stone steps into the very heart of their own city, beloved Assisi, they reached the marketplace. It had been open since dawn and most of the stall holders had left. Those that remained huddled on the shady side of the marketplace or round the fountain that dripped water into a stone trough. A few sad-looking animals: chickens, a rabbit, a canary or two, drooped inside cages. Francis looked at them and then quickly away again. The memory of a beating he'd had when he'd opened a cage door to let free a bird was too recent to repeat.

To divert himself, he kicked at an old turnip rolling across the stone floor and soon the boys were divided into teams and sending their turnip ball flying across the square. But it was too hot to play for long and besides they were hungry so, after splashing water at each other and being cursed by an old man for wetting him too, they split up for their homes.

Francis kicked the turnip all the way to his front door and, by the time he'd arrived, it looked to him just like a Saracen's head.

Francis' family was already eating by the time he arrived. His father, Pietro Bernardino, sat at one end of the table; his mother, Pica at the other; his younger brothers and sister in between. Pietro was a rich merchant who bought and sold fine cloth and in a few years' time Francis would be expected to help in the business. Pietro was a strong, heavy-set man, unlike Francis who was small for his age and fragile-looking, with big dark eyes. Making a hasty sign of the cross, he grabbed a chunk of bread and broke it into the thick vegetable soup in his place.

As the years passed, little changed in Francis' life. Just as he had been a leader as a child, he became leader of the group of rich young men who did as little work as they could by day and spent the night feasting and drinking. Francis always

loved beauty, whether it was the
scarlet poppies and blue cornflowers
that grew on the edge of the fields
or the red and blue flag of Assisi
which hung on the churches and on
the battlements. He designed for
himself splendid clothes which his
father was willing to pay for because
he could not help being proud of
his charming, brilliant son who,
although only a merchant's son,
was accepted among the nobles.

The money would be well spent
if Francis brought honour to the
house of Bernardino by marrying
one of the fine young ladies that
were sisters to the friends he
caroused with. These ladies, like the
heroines of the love-songs, spent
their days quietly in household
tasks, drying herbs to spread among
the linen, embroidering exquisite
hangings. On Sunday mornings,
they could be seen on their way to
mass, veils over their coiled and
plaited hair, sumptuously dressed in
silk and velvet. Or, in the summer,
they might be glimpsed through
a partly open door, seated in a
courtyard filled with flowering
shrubs and shady trees and a glitter-
ing fountain. These were the sort of
ladies Pietro and Pica dreamt of as
a wife for their eldest son.

But Francis' extravagance was not just for himself. One day he was unrolling a length of cloth for a buyer when a beggar pulled at his arm. Assisi, as the whole of Italy, was filled with beggars, usually sick and often maimed or deformed. The most frightening kind of beggars, the lepers, were not allowed inside cities.

Ordinary beggars mixed with the crowded streets and, pleadingly, held out a hand. That was accepted. But for a beggar to come into a shop was considered quite wrong. 'Give me money, in the name of Christ!' pleaded the beggar and, even before he'd finished, Francis had chased him away. Then, in another second, as if struck by a new thought, Francis had dropped the cloth and crying out, 'Where is my heart!' he rushed down the street and pressed coins into the hands of the very surprised beggar. From that moment on Francis never refused anyone who begged in the name of Christ.

By now Francis was twenty and, although he didn't yet know it, his life was soon going to change completely. Across the valley, the high ramparts and watch-towers of Perugia disguised preparation for war. German nobles who had

been chased out of Assisi a few years earlier, had persuaded Perugia to declare war on her neighbour. Hastily, Assisi began to raise her own army; all the men between eighteen and sixty were called up. The poor became foot soldiers. Those who were rich enough to buy a horse and the silver shield and helmet of a knight prepared themselves as if they were one of King Arthur's knights, the heroes of their troubadour ballads.

Francis was one of these would-be heroes; his mind was filled with romantic dreams as the army left the safe walls of Assisi and crossed the plain before climbing again to the looming towers of Perugia. Assisi had been joined by other small towns: Foligno, Nocera, Spello, Risciano and Bastia, and their banners fluttered gaily above the excited horses and eager soldiers who carried battle-axes and pikes, swords and daggers. The noise of neighing horses was punctuated by the high scream of the trumpets and the cheers of the children who ran after them. From the ramparts mothers and sisters, wives and lovers watched their menfolk go. Francis' mother, Pica, held on to her younger sons, glad they were too young to fight. She could not guess it would be a year before they saw Francis again.

The battle was short and bloody. The giant Perugia easily swallowed little Assisi, despite her brave allies. Many were killed and it was only Francis' dress as a knight that saved his life. Unlike foot soldiers who were killed without mercy, knights were taken alive because it was assumed their families were rich enough to pay a ransom.

Francis and his companions were thrown into a dungeon far below the streets where it was dark day and night, and the walls were always damp even in the height of summer. Instead of the flowers and trees that Francis so loved there was only mildew; instead of birds and deer and rabbits, there were mice and rats. Despite this, Francis was always good-humoured and made an especial friend of a fellow prisoner who was disliked by everybody else because they suspected him of being a traitor.

A year is a very long time to be cut off from the brightness of life and when Francis was finally ransomed and allowed back to Assisi, his parents saw that he had changed. At first they imagined it was only weakness after his captivity because he immediately fell ill with a high fever. But when he did recover, he no longer seemed to enjoy his usual round of pleasure. Often he went off to be alone, taking long walks outside the city walls. There, he passed a leper hospital before climbing up Mount Subasio on whose slopes Assisi was built. His father couldn't help being disappointed that he took even less interest in the cloth business than before.

Surprisingly, Francis still seemed to dream of heroic deeds. Twice he set out for the wars. The first time he got hardly further than the city walls before he gave away the armour to a young knight who was not so well provided for and Francis thought worthier than himself. It was as if something was pulling Francis back from the fighting. The second time he rode as far as the Southern city of Spoleto where he camped with the other soldiers outside the town walls.

That night, as the soldiers slept, exhausted after a long day's riding, Francis alone stayed awake. He looked at the pale tendrils of smoke from their fire rising up in the black sky and suddenly heard a voice speaking in his ear. At first he thought it was one of his friends but he twisted round to look and there was nobody.

'Francis, who can do better for you, the Lord or the servant?' The voice was thrilling and unlike anything he had ever heard . . .

Francis answered, 'The Lord.'

'Why then,' continued the voice, 'do you leave the Lord to follow the servant?'

With a feeling of terror and amazement, Francis realised this was God speaking to him, so he whispered, 'Lord, what would you have me do?'

And God told him, 'Go back home and you will be told what to do.'

As soon as a streaky dawn silhouetted the city ahead of him, Francis said goodbye to his astonished companions, mounted his horse and rode for home. There he would await God's message.

Back in Assisi, Francis tried not to listen when people called him a coward. Sometimes now he climbed up to caves high on the mountainside which were used by holy men and hermits and there in the peaceful darkness he prayed for understanding. He still spent time with his friends in town, although they were increasingly bewildered by his strange behaviour.

One of his best friends liked to accompany Francis, hoping he'd find deer or perhaps wild boar to shoot with his arrows. As spring greened the trees, he watched Francis sighing mournfully as he came out of a cave and began to tease him, 'I know your problem. You're in love. That's why you're doing all this sighing and groaning. Soon we'll see you married to a fine lady.'

Francis stepped close to his friend and looked into his smiling face. 'You are wrong,' he said. 'I am in love with a bride more beautiful than you could ever imagine and her name is Lady Poverty.'

Now Francis began to give away not only money but also the clothes he was wearing. One day when his father was away he invited beggars into his home so that they could share in the good food and comfortable surroundings he had enjoyed all his life.

Yet this was only play-acting and Francis was still the spoilt son of a rich man who hated dirt and discomfort and had a particular horror of lepers. One summer's afternoon, he was riding in the woods below Assisi when he heard a bell ringing which signalled the approach of a leper. He was about to change direction like any sensible man, when he suddenly realised that here was an opportunity to prove he really did want to follow Jesus' teachings. Rushing up to the amazed leper, he took him in his arms, filthy rags, stinking, suppurating sores, and kissed him as if he were a long lost brother. Now he gave not just to the poor but to the lepers too. He had become the friend and comfort of society's outcasts.

Francis was seldom at home and, as the stories of his strange behaviour increased, his parents began to believe he was losing his mind. Pietro had given up thinking he would ever take over the business. After all, Francis spent nearly as much time giving away Pietro's money as Pietro spent making it! Luckily, his second son was dutiful in the way his father understood, so Francis was free to go out of the city and pray quietly in his favourite place, the old church of St. Damiano. Although it was almost in ruins, a huge painted crucifix still hung above the altar. Sometimes, Francis spent so many hours there and kept so still that the birds who lived in the woods flew into the roofless building and made nests in the column above his head.

One evening he had stayed late and a moon shone down onto the cross. Its gleam caught Francis' eye and he looked up. To his amazement, he saw the lips of Christ move.

'Francis,' He said, 'go and repair my house, which, as you see, is fallen into ruin.'

Now Francis knew how to start his new life. But, as always, there was the question of money. The next morning, taking advantage of his father's absence, Francis took a bale of expensive scarlet cloth to the market at Foligno. But instead of bringing home the bag of money he made from the sale, he took it to St. Damiano's where he tried to give it to a monk who acted as caretaker.

'The money is not yours to give,' insisted the old priest. In confusion, Francis flung the money onto a dusty ledge.

Of course the moment Pietro came home he discovered his son's latest act of madness – as he saw it. Enraged, he went up to St. Damiano's where Francis was

living like a beggar and began to beat him and yell accusations, as if he were crazy himself. His servants tied up Francis and led him back to Assisi where he was chained and locked in a cellar underneath the large house. Francis must have felt as if he were a prisoner in Perugia again.

But Francis' loving mother, Pica, could not bear to see her son treated like a common criminal and, as soon as her husband had left the city on business, she let out Francis. Despite her pleadings, he left at once for St. Damiano's to continue his life of poverty, prayer and helping the poor.

Pietro's rage was even greater on his return. He wanted Francis tried in a court of law. But Francis insisted that the Bishop should be his judge because he had acted out of religious belief. The trial took place in the palace in the centre of Assisi where Bishop Guido lived. A curious audience gathered inside while outside the poor huddled along the walls. The Bishop did not hesitate. He told Francis, 'God does not want stolen money. The cloth you sold belonged to your father and so does the money.' Francis did not hesitate either. First he flung down the bag of money and then he tore off his clothes and tossed them towards his father. He stood alone, a thin, pale figure, dressed only in a hair shirt. The audience had not expected such good entertainment as this and they were all agog.

Francis cried, 'I have given back to my father everything that was his, even to the clothes I stood up in. From now on,' he continued, 'I may freely say "My Father who is in Heaven" instead of my father Pietro Bernardino!'

Some people laughed but the Bishop understood that Francis wanted to dedicate his life to God and, opening wide his great cloak, invited Francis to shelter there. From that day onwards, Francis the rich man's son had died and Francis, the beggar and holy man was born.

So Francis must rebuild the old church of St. Damiano's without any money. The only answer was to turn himself into a builder. Soon he had taught himself how to lay one heavy stone on top of another. Now he went into the city to beg for stone as well as bread, ignoring the children's cries of 'Il Pazzo!' - the madman - whenever they saw him.

When Francis had finished building St. Damiano's, he turned to another ruin, the little church at the Portiuncula, called St. Mary of the Angels. Not long after Francis had finished the two churches, he was attending a service in St. Damiano when the priest read this passage from the New Testament: 'And as you travel, say that the kingdom of heaven is at hand. Heal the sick, cleanse the lepers, raise the dead . . . Take neither gold nor silver nor any money for your journey. Wear no shoes, carry no food but preach repentance . . .' These were the words Jesus had spoken to his disciples and Francis knew without any doubt that they were also a command for him. To the surprise of the priest, he cried out, 'This is what I wish, this is what I am seeking, this I long to do!' Straightaway, he took off his sandals and, painting a cross on his tunic, started off on a new life as a travelling preacher.

WHEREVER FRANCIS WAS, IN THE SQUARE in front of the cathedral in Assisi or in other towns down in the valleys or perched on the hillsides round about, he began by saying, 'Peace be with you.' He was always cheerful, friendly and spoke with such simplicity and directness that he drew bigger and bigger audiences. Some wanted to do more than merely listen to him speak.

Two new friends, Bernard da Quintavalle and Peter Cathani were both rich men, a business man and a lawyer, better educated than Francis. The three young men prayed together in St. Georgio's church where Francis had been to school and occasionally Francis spent the night at Bernard's grand house which was not far from his own family home. Bernard noticed, however, that Francis used most of the night for praying. He knelt, bare knees on the cold stone floor, and repeated over and over again, 'My God and my all.'

In a few weeks Bernard had made up his mind to join Francis and a new scandal hit Assisi. Half the population raced along to the square of St. Georgio to watch another Francis-induced madness as a rich citizen gave away to the poor all his money, fine clothes and possessions.

As the number of Francis' followers grew to eight, they built a simple hut in the woods and worked in the fields. But, whenever they were travelling, they still begged for their living. They walked everywhere, as Jesus did, their bare feet gradually hardening over the rocky paths. In the summer, they tried to keep to the woodlands where the trees shaded them from the boiling sun, in the icy winter, they stayed in the valleys and sheltered in a shepherd's hut or a cattle shed.

As soon as there were twelve brothers, like Jesus' twelve apostles, Francis decided it was time to visit the Pope, Innocent III, and ask that they could be recognised as a proper order. The Pope held court in Rome with as much grandeur as a king. Anyone but Francis would have been afraid to approach such a formidable person but Francis always looked on things in the simplest way and, since he was determined his order should be part of the Catholic Church, he went directly to its head.

Assisi and Rome are over a hundred miles apart which makes it a very long walk. It was a battered and dirty Francis who, with his companions, finally entered the walls of Rome. Without pausing to wash or take advice, Francis rushed straight to the palace where the Pope lived and, by some strange chance, found him, all on his own, pacing up and down the Gallery of Mirrors. Francis

flung himself at his feet and, with his usual enthusiasm, poured out his plans for a new order based on the teaching of Jesus, with poverty a very important part of it.

Perhaps understandably, the Pope was horrified at the wild figure in front of him and called his guards to throw him out, advising Francis in passing that he looked more suited to a pigsty than a palace.

The story of Francis might have ended here except that, by coincidence, Bishop Guido was also in Rome and decided to help Francis. The second time round Francis was given an official audience with Innocent III who sat on his throne with all his cardinals dressed in rich velvet and fur around him. The Pope listened carefully to Francis and said that he would give him a decision the next morning. That night as the Pope lay asleep he had a dream that the great church of St. John the Baptist and St. John the Evangelist was cracking apart and that he could only watch as it fell apart. Suddenly he saw a little brown-robed figure whom he recognised as the would-be monk, Francis, crossing the piazza towards it. All alone, he put his shoulder against the crumbling walls and stopped the church from falling.

The next day the Pope welcomed Francis and gave him permission to found an order of friars, called the Fratres Minores or Little Brothers.

The band of brothers left the marble halls of Rome for the long, hard journey home. The battered hut outside Assisi was so small for so many that Francis had the brothers' names painted on the rafters so that they knew what order to squeeze in. Inside it was uncomfortable; outside it was dangerous. Not just because of the wolves in winter and snakes in summer but because many battles were being fought up and down the land.

Although Francis was well known now, he still lived like a beggar and insisted that his friars only accepted just enough food to keep them alive. So they were often very hungry and one night a young brother woke up in such pain he thought he was dying. His groans woke Francis who immediately prepared a little meal which he shared with him so that he would not feel ashamed of his weakness. Francis told him kindly, 'We must each eat what we need to do our work, for the Lord is merciful and does not want useless sacrifices.'

As it happened they were not to stay in their cramped home much longer because early one morning the monks were woken by a loud braying noise followed by a donkey stamping through the door. He was being driven in by a peasant shouting, 'Get along in with you. This is just the right stabling for you.' Francis liked the donkey well enough but could not stand the rudeness of his owner so he led out the brothers in search of another home.

When the Benedictine monks offered him the use of the Portiuncula as a base, it seemed as if the angry peasant had served a very useful purpose. Now, as the order expanded more and more, they had space for a proper headquarters. Near the church of St. Mary of the Angels, they built little huts or cells, made more of mud than anything else because Francis would not use anything as expensive and lasting as stone. Around the cells he planted a hedge and within the hedge the friars grew vegetables and brightly coloured flowers. Francis always loved flowers. He said, 'Whoever looks at them will be put in mind of heaven.'

It certainly wasn't very heavenly inside the huts, with no chairs or tables and a pile of straw for a bed. But to Francis and his companions, it was just what they needed: a peaceful home from which they could go out on their journeys to preach in other towns and villages. Besides, Francis always felt happy to be near natural things. It made him feel closer to God who had created the trees and the birds and the beasts just as He had created man.

Francis so loved the tall trees which grew thickly round the Portiuncula, that he would never let a whole tree be cut down. In the same way, he taught his companions to respect the streams which ran down from the mountains and which gave them sparkling water to wash in and to drink. He told them water was a symbol of purity. He even respected the rocks which made walking so difficult because they represented God's mighty strength. Above all, he treated animals as kindly as if they were his brothers and sisters. Perhaps this was why even the wildest animals trusted him.

In his cell, Francis kept a pet grasshopper who woke him every morning at just the right time for him to sing his first prayers of the morning. After a while, Francis invited Sister Grasshopper to join in with their prayers and she did so enthusiastically. Francis also had a pet rabbit who came to live with him after he had escaped a trap. But Francis' first love was always the birds who seemed to follow him everywhere.

One late summer day when the cornfields had been newly cut and a huge gathering of birds was pecking at the fallen seed while others swirled above or made sudden attacking raids, Francis left his companions who were walking with him along the path and dashed eagerly into the field.

'Peace be with you!' he cried to the rooks and pigeons, starlings and crows, and, instead of rising and flying away, they sat waiting for him. Francis was filled with joy and began talking to them just as if they were people in a city square.

'My brother birds,' he said, 'your Creator has given you feathers for clothing, wings for flying and the wide sky for your home. You are the luckiest creatures in the world and should love God and thank him for his kindness.'

As Francis talked the birds stretched out their necks towards him, spread their wings and opened their beaks as if they understood every word. Francis walked among them, his tunic brushing their feathers and, as he walked, he blessed them and only when he had seen to every one did he give them permission to fly away. Off they went, North, South, East, West, forming a huge dark cross in the sky.

'Dearest brothers,' said Francis, returning to his companions, 'I can't think why I have never preached to the birds before - they are such good listeners!'

Usually, Francis welcomed any bird that came to perch on a tree above his head or dashed down to peck the bread from his hands. But, on one occasion,

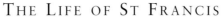

he had to speak severely to a flock of swallows. He was trying to preach a sermon in the town of Alviano but the swallows were making such a racket as they built their nests that no-one could hear a word Francis was saying.

Raising his hands to them in his friendly way, he reasoned, 'My sister swallows, you've had your say for a good long time, surely you can see it is now my turn to speak.' At once the swallows became silent.

Francis seemed able to charm every creature and every person he met. However there was a sterner side to his character. One of the rules of the Franciscan order was absolute obedience because that helped the brothers to become humbler and closer to God. One brother, called Rufino, was a nobleman from Assisi and found day to day life in the Portiuncula very difficult. The thing he most dreaded was speaking in front of a crowd and probably being mocked by the sort of rough person he had been brought up to despise.

Francis, deciding to confront Rufino's weakness, commanded him to go and preach in the cathedral at Assisi. Rufino was horrified and pleaded, 'Reverend Father, please take pity and do not send me.'

But Francis became even firmer, 'Because you haven't obeyed me at once, I shall make it even worse for you. Take off all your clothes except your breeches and preach like that.'

So poor Rufino stood in the pulpit of the cathedral more or less naked and his old friends and the rabble from the streets and the children laughed at him and said to each other, 'These monks have done so many hard penances they have lost their wits!'

Back at the Portiuncula, Francis imagined what his friend was going through and suddenly he was overcome with shame at the harshness of his punishment. Throwing off his own clothes, Francis rushed into town and took his place beside Rufino so now there were two crazy men for the people to mock. But Francis' words about the teaching of Jesus were so persuasive that tears of laughter changed to tears of emotion.

AMONG THE CROWD IN THE CATHEDRAL WAS a young and beautiful nobleman's daughter called Clare who was well known for her generosity and kindness to the poor. As a child of eleven she had seen Francis throw his clothes at his father and afterwards she never missed an opportunity to hear him speak.

All Francis' closest companions, the friars of the First Order, were, of course, men but some women did come to visit the Portiuncula. Although they were not allowed to enter beyond the boundary hedge, Francis went out to talk to them. One of these women was Clare. Now she had grown up, her parents expected her to marry into a rich and aristocratic family like their own and be content with bringing up her children and running the household. But Clare had no interest in any of these things, not her fine clothes, nor her fine surroundings, nor the handsome young men who came to court her. She wanted to serve God in the same way Francis had chosen, with prayer, poverty and in humble service to the sick and poor.

All this she confided in Francis as they walked under the great vaulting trees of the forest. Sometimes he carried his pet rabbit and sometimes he was followed by a row of baby robins who had adopted him as their father. Just as he could understand the hearts of such wild creatures, so he understood this highborn lady and knew that her need to escape the life she was leading was true and strong.

By now Clare's father had died and her uncle, who was a bully of a man, had become her guardian. Clare knew she could never persuade him to let her leave so she determined to run away. On Palm Sunday, Clare attended the long mass sung in Latin just as she did each year. She wore a scarlet robe with a jewelled belt, embroidered shoes on her feet and an elaborate head-dress over her golden hair. She was the most beautiful woman there but her cheeks were pale and her hands trembled. She was so nervous that she did not have the strength to go up to the altar to receive an olive branch as was the custom, and Bishop Guido himself brought it to her.

But that same evening this slim, nineteen-year-old girl who had been protected all her life, secretly met her cousin Bianca and together they hurried through the dark streets of the city and out into the olive groves and woods beyond. As they reached the Portiuncula, they saw flaming torches and heard voices singing and the friars came towards them in a welcoming procession.

They were led to the church of St. Mary of the Angels where Clare made her vows just as the monks did, had her shining hair cut to her scalp, and was given the hooded tunic with a cross on the front, just like the brothers.

That night Clare stayed near with Francis and the other friars in the church. But as a woman, Clare could not live among the friars so she moved on to a Benedictine convent. As soon as she had arrived her uncle came to snatch her back but she clung to the altar and refused to leave. 'Look!' she cried and pushing back the hood, showed her shaven head. 'Now you can see I'm a bride of Christ!'

Horrified, her uncle gave up and went away. After a while Clare was joined by her fourteen-year-old sister Agnes and once more their furious uncle came, this time with a band of armed men, including their brothers and cousins. Again they could not budge Clare but they snatched up Agnes and carried her bodily down the mountainside. But God was watching over Agnes because after a while she became as heavy as lead weights and the men could not carry her any further and the two sisters were reunited.

It took a year for Clare to find a place where she could have a convent of her own, run on the same lines as the Franciscans. The Benedictines decided to give her the old church of St. Damiano, which Francis had restored, with a building attached where she could live. Happily for Francis and Clare, this was very close to the Portiuncula.

Clare's order became the Second Order of St Francis, often called the Poor Clares. It grew quickly and later her mother, Ortelena, joined with a third sister, Beatrice.

Once Clare was established at St. Damiano's, she remained there all her life. Francis, on the other hand, took the paths through the countryside, from walled town to walled town, Brother Ever-Glad as he was nicknamed, striding through meadows and woods, across streams, singing his favourite songs.

At this time so many people were attracted to Francis and his teaching that he established a Third Order for the ordinary people of Assisi who could not leave their families or their work but still wanted to be a part of the great Franciscan community.

ROME WAS THE CENTRE OF THE CATHOLIC CHURCH because the Pope lived there and Francis needed to visit the city at least once a year. He usually stayed with a noblewoman called Giacoma di Settesoli. Her husband had died when she was still young and left her with large estates to look after and two little sons to bring up. Francis helped her to use her power properly and she was so sensible and became such close a friend that he called her Brother Giacoma.

Giacoma gave Francis comforts he would not accept from anyone else; she even cooked him a special marzipan cake, called 'frangipani' which you can still buy in Italy today. Francis, in his turn, gave her a lamb he'd saved from slaughter which he thought would make a very nice pet. This became awkward when the lamb grew into a large sheep but Giacoma, who was a practical sort of person, sheared its wool, spun it into yarn and wove the yarn into cloth.

There were special difficulties for Francis in Rome because he was invited to attend all kinds of grand events which did not fit in with his ideas of poverty and

simplicity. On one occasion he was due at a feast given by a Cardinal called Ugolino. Francis was so shocked by what he saw being prepared, the whole animals roasted on a spit, the flagons of expensive wines, the very things he had enjoyed as a young man and given up, that he did not take his place of honour beside the Cardinal. Instead, he went out on the streets and begged scraps from house to house as was his custom.

When Francis had enough bits of old bread, stale cheese and hard salami, he returned to the feast, sat in his place, and laid out these scraps in front of him. Poor Cardinal Ugolino felt shamed in front of all his guests and shamed, also, that a guest of his had been seen begging on the streets. But such was Francis' holiness and sincerity that Ugolino quickly forgave him and realised that he had been taught a lesson in humility.

Francis never allowed ordinary feelings of embarrassment or even fear to affect his behaviour. One cold winter he was staying in Gubbio when he noticed

to his surprise that no-one ventured outside the city walls unless they were in large groups or very well armed.

'What is it you're so afraid of?' he asked. He was told that a huge wolf had carried off their lambs and threatened their little children so that no-one felt safe by day or by night. Now a lot of the older and frailer citizens hardly dared leave the city at all.

'Show me where this monster lives!' cried Francis - a little as if he were St. George facing the Dragon - and, without hesitation and with no defence except his faith in God, he set off to find the wolf in its den. At the beginning he was accompanied by crowds of men, women and children but by the time he had arrived at the thickest part of the forest where the bright sunlight had turned to deep green shade, only the bravest men and boys were still with him. They watched from a safe distance as Francis strode forward. Horrified, they watched the wolf leap out with gaping jaws.

'Come closer, Brother Wolf,' said Francis without flinching and he made the sign of the cross over the snarling animal. 'In the name of Jesus, I command you not to hurt me nor anyone ever again.'

At these words, the wolf closed his snapping jaws and laid down at Francis' feet. 'You have been behaving very badly,' continued Francis severely, 'killing your fellow beasts and even man who is made in the image of God, and you deserve the gallows just as much as any murderer. Quite understandably, the whole city is out for your blood. But I want to make peace with you so if you promise to behave yourself I will make sure you are never chased again by man or dog. And moreover, I will see that you always have food to eat because I know it was hunger that made you behave so badly. Do I have your promise?'

To everyone's astonishment, the wolf bowed his head in agreement and then lifted his paw and put it into Francis' hand.

'Excellent,' said Francis. 'Now you may come with me into Gubbio and confirm this peace in front of all the citizens.'

Word soon got around that Francis was coming back into the city with the wicked wolf and a huge crowd had gathered in the main square by the time Francis walked in, with the wolf trotting at his side as tame as a pet lamb. Francis took up position in the centre of the square while the wolf sat meekly at his side.

'I have brought you peace,' he shouted to the crowd. 'You need fear nothing

now except the flames of hell. The wolf will not hurt you, and you on your side must not hurt him but must see that he does not go hungry.' He turned to the wolf. 'Is that not right, Brother Wolf?'

Once again, the wolf bowed his head and placed his paw in Francis' hand so that everyone could believe in the change in his character. From that day onwards, Brother Wolf lived in the city, going like the monks to ask politely for food and being treated kindly by everyone because he reminded them of Francis. When Brother Wolf died two years later he was buried under the stone floor of a church and, about a hundred and fifty years ago, his skull was uncovered, which proves he truly existed.

As the Franciscan brothers grew in number from twelve to a hundred and twelve and from hundreds to thousands, Francis spent much of his time travelling from one friary to another, preaching in all the great cities of Italy. But despite his dedicated life, he still had not given up his childhood ambition to be part of the crusade to convert the heathens. Twice he set out on expeditions: once to Spain and once to Syria. On the first occasion he fell ill and on the second his ship was wrecked on a distant shore. Nevertheless he had not given up, and one bright morning he arrived at St. Damiano's and announced to Clare that he was off to convert the Sultan in Syria.

Francis set sail from Ancona, picking his tall-masted ship from the hundreds that filled this busy Italian port. The blue sea with its white-crested waves was an exciting change from the green hills and yellow plains that he knew so well. The journey took many months and sometimes the sky was black and the ship dashed across the water, sliding up and down mountainous waves. At other times, the sky and sea were as blue and calm as each other and the ship seemed to be asleep, while the mocking seagulls nested in the rigging.

Eventually, Francis arrived safely at his destination, the port of Acre in Syria. His plan was simple enough: he would go straight to the Egyptian leader Malek-el-Kamil, the Sultan, and point out the merits of Christianity. He wanted to bring peace to the region because the Crusaders, with red crosses on their tunics, were engaged in a war against the Sultan. They had already been camped for a year outside the city of Damietta, which was built on the mouth of the Nile, and the Christians had been twice defeated in their efforts to take the city when Francis arrived.

It was August and a boiling hot sun beat down on the desert all around and the rows of tents which stretched for miles across the sandy ground. Damietta, a white fortified city, gleamed on the horizon. From the distance it looked like a pretty toy and not a place filled with fierce soldiers with curving scimitars and machines to throw rocks at invaders. Shortly after Francis' arrival the Christian armies which were made up from soldiers from many European countries including Britain, were thrown back for the third time and many thousands of men were killed or captured or horribly maimed.

Francis was horrified by this pointless loss of life but he was just as shocked to find that these soldiers who wore the cross of Jesus so proudly often were no better than the barbarians they wanted to convert. This strengthened his resolve to cross enemy lines and speak directly to the Sultan.

Naturally, everyone thought he was mad and reminded him of what any sensible person knew, that the Saracens cut off the head of any Christian who tried to enter their camp. But Francis took no notice and, choosing a brother called Illuminato as his companion, set off across the desert. First it was very, very hot, the light striking onto Francis' eyes like knives; then, as the sun sank in a fiery ball and a cool moon rose, it became so cold that both men shivered in their ragged tunics.

To cheer themselves up, they sang a psalm which begins, 'Though I walk through the valley of the shadow of death, I shall fear no evil . . .' Eventually they reached the Saracen sentries and shouted over and over the only Arab word they knew, 'Soldan!' which means 'Sultan'. Perhaps the sentries thought they were messengers for the Sultan, because, although the two friars were beaten and bound in chains, they were not killed but thrown into prison. A few days later they were dragged in front of the Sultan.

To amuse himself and his court, the Sultan had commanded a rug patterned in crosses to be placed before them. 'If they walk over it, it will be an insult to their God and if they refuse, it will be an insult to me,' he told his courtiers.

But Francis walked over the rug without hesitation. 'There were three crosses when our Christ died,' he informed the Sultan. 'Our cross is the cross that Jesus died on but *you* may have the thieves' crosses to do with what you like.'

Despite being badly bruised and sick with a fever, Francis talked to the Sultan for many hours. He talked of his feelings for a loving God and the Sultan who was a deeply religious man, although he believed in Allah, listened very carefully. In fact the two men found so much to discuss and Francis and Iluminato stayed there so long that their companions back in the camp began to believe they had been beheaded, as predicted.

They had almost lost hope of ever seeing them again when two ragged figures emerged out of the desert. Francis had not been able to persuade the Sultan to become a Christian but he had done something as bold and brave as any soldier.

In the course of his visit the Sultan's brother had given Francis a special pass which allowed him to enter Jerusalem and see the place where Jesus had taught and died. So Francis travelled down from Syria to the Holy Land. He visited

Bethlehem, the hill-top village where Jesus was born and walked the beautiful hills of Galilee which had not changed since Jesus walked over them a thousand years before.

By now Francis had been away from the Portiuncula for over a year. He might have stayed away longer except that a messenger arrived from Italy to summon him home. There were problems with the Franciscan Order he had founded and he was needed to sort things out.

This return to Italy was a miserable time for Francis. He should have been happy to see his beloved Portiuncula, to take his favourite walks through the countryside which often led him to St. Damiano where Clare lived with the other Sisters. But after his long absence in the East, Francis had problems that even Clare could not solve. Two of the Brothers had taken control of the Franciscan Order and were trying to run it like other orders, with fine houses to live in, elegant books to read and good food and wine.

Francis tried his best to make the changes back towards poverty but his health was bad and his eyes had never properly recovered from the blinding light in the desert so that he could only see the brightest colours. Now he spent less time in the big cities and more in the little friaries, like Grecchi in the hills above the valley of Riete. Sometimes he lived like a hermit for days or even weeks at a time in

a cave high up on the mountainside. One winter when the trees were bare and snow covered the highest slopes, he was reminded of the cave he had seen at Bethlehem where Jesus was born and he decided to invent a new sort of Christmas worship for the children living in the villages around. He arranged for an ox and an ass to be led into the cave and the manger to be filled with sweet - smelling hay so it was just like the one Mary had used as a crib for the baby Jesus. Instead of holding the first Christmas service in the church as usual, he held it in this cave at midnight.

A long procession wound up the mountainside, each person carrying a candle or flaming torch so that the trees were lit up as if it were day. As they walked they sang hymns and their joyful singing echoed backwards and forwards across the hill-tops. As many as could fit crowded into the cave and some said afterwards that, as the host was raised up with the words, 'This is my body,' they could see a new-born baby tucked up in the manger.

There was one place even more isolated and peaceful than the hermitage above Grecchi. That was a mountain-top called La Verna which Francis had been given some years earlier by a rich admirer. In the summer Francis set out with seven monks, including Leo, Angelo and Illuminato and started the long climb upwards. Although Francis was only in his early forties, his hard life and his illness made him seem a much older man. As usual now a donkey was found for him to ride and when the animal's owner discovered who would be the rider, he wasn't at all overawed but told Francis, 'You have the reputation of being a great and holy man so just mind you don't disappoint us.' Instead of being cross at such disrespect from a crusty old peasant, Francis dismounted from the donkey and, kissing the man's feet, thanked him for the reminder.

It was a hot day in August and, after a few hours, the difficult peasant began to complain, 'Ah me, I'll die of thirst if I don't get a drink soon.' Once more Francis dismounted but this time he knelt down in prayer. After a few minutes he told the peasant, 'Go to that rock over there and you will find running water.' The peasant obeyed him even though he knew for certain there was no water thereabouts yet, to his amazement, he saw a spring gushing from the hard rock which was as pure and sweet as any water he had ever tasted. So on they travelled until they reached the top of the mountain where Francis meant to spend the summer months. They built little huts out of saplings for shelter and Francis chose to put his under a beech tree. They had not brought much to eat or drink but soon Count Orlando, who had given Francis the mountain, heard of the friars' arrival. He left his castle and brought them bread and wine but when he wanted to add luxuries to make their stay more comfortable, Francis reminded him of their vows of poverty and refused.

At first Francis was happy but after a while he wanted to be entirely on his own. One day he was wandering round the back of the mountain when he saw ahead of him a deep chasm. He fetched some of the other brothers and together they laid a fallen tree trunk across the chasm to act as a bridge.

'Now,' Francis told Leo, 'when I'm on the other side I want visits from no-one except you once a day to bring me bread and water. Come at night-time so we can say our prayers together but if, when you call across the chasm, I do not call back "Come!" then leave me alone.'

So Francis lived apart from the brothers in this wild and desolate place. But he was not entirely alone because a Falcon built her nest near his cell. In the early morning, she woke him for his prayers by singing and beating her wings on the door. Francis called Sister Falcon his 'clock' and was glad to have such a cheerful and useful companion.

Each night Leo brought supplies as agreed until one moonlit night he called out but Francis did not reply 'Come'. Worried that he might have fallen sick, Leo crossed the bridge all the same and then stopped in amazement. Far brighter than the full moon, scarlet tongues of flame poured down from the sky to where Francis stood, arms outstretched.

Leo stared until the flames returned to the heavens and then, ashamed of spying, tried to creep away without being seen. But Francis heard the crisp leaves rustling under his feet and turned in his direction. Francis' eyes were so bad now that it took him a moment or two to see his friend but then he spoke to him kindly, 'Ah, my little sheep, so you couldn't resist following me.'

It was not until Francis left his solitary home across the chasm and rejoined the friars that he showed Leo what had happened to him that strange moonlit night. His hands and his feet had been pierced with wounds just as Jesus had suffered when he was nailed to the cross. And there was an even deeper wound in his side in the place where the soldier had put his lance into Jesus' side. Francis bore these marks for the rest of his life. He tried to hide them so that the world

shouldn't know and, although they hurt terribly, he felt honoured to suffer from the same wounds as Jesus. As summer turned to winter, Francis and the other friars came down from the mountain. At night heavy dew soaked the ground they slept on and in the morning the trees were shrouded in dank mists. They were heading for the Portiuncula but sometimes the wind and rain washed away their path and sent stones rattling down ahead of them. They were glad to reach the bottom and find friendly villages and towns and monasteries where they could spend a night or two.

Francis had always had the gift of healing and it seemed as his body grew weaker, his spirit grew even stronger. Soon it was rumoured that Francis had the marks of Jesus' stigmata on his hands and feet and that he only had to touch a sick child - or a man or a woman - for that person to be miraculously cured. There was a particular friar who writhed continuously with a violent epilepsy so that his body was twisted into knots. Hearing about this, Francis blessed a piece of bread and sent it to him. After one bite, the friar's body became relaxed and healed.

Francis had never been the least bit interested in the suffering of his poor body, which he nick-named Brother Ass, and, after his return to the Portiuncula he continued to preach in the nearby villages. He was so famous now that the children welcomed him with cries of 'Il Santo! Il Santo!' - just as when he was young, other children cried: 'Il Pazzo! Il Pazzo!' The madman had become a saint.

But his eyes were becoming worse every day and Brother Elias, who now ran the order, finally managed to convince Francis that Brother Ass deserved some help. 'God created medicine out of the earth,' he said, 'and the wise man should not shrink from it.'

So Francis agreed to go to Rieti where his friend and protector, Cardinal Ugolino, was staying. It was spring, a good time for travelling, and on his way across the hillside, Francis called in at St. Damiano's to say goodbye to Clare. He meant to stay only for a day but he became so ill that he could not leave for many weeks.

Clare and the other sisters looked after him lovingly. They made a bed for him on a little terraced garden because, although he could see very little now, he liked the feel of the sun on his face and the sweet smell of the flowers around

him. Despite his pain, he felt very happy in this peaceful place. One morning, just as the sun was rising and a few early birds were making fluttering shadows across his eyelids, he pulled himself upright so that he would feel closer to the dawn of another beautiful day. He had always been aware of the glory of God's creation but his suffering seemed to make his feelings even stronger. Raising himself higher, he began singing as he used to when young:

"Praise to Thee, my Lord, for all thy creatures,
Above all Brother Sun,
Who brings us the day and lends us his light.
Lovely is he, radiant with great splendour,
And speaks to us of Thee,
Most High!

Praise to Thee, my Lord, for Sister Moon and all the stars,
Which Thou has set in the heavens,
Clear, precious and fair.

Praise to Thee, my Lord, for Brother Wind,
For air and cloud, for calm and all weather,
By which Thou supportest life in all Thy creatures.

Praise to Thee, my Lord, for Sister Water,
Who is so useful and humble,
Precious and pure.

Praise to Thee, my Lord, for Brother Fire,
By whom Thou lightest the night;
He is lovely and kind, mighty and strong.

Praise to Thee, my Lord, for our sister, Mother Earth,
Who comforts and looks after us,
And brings forth fruits, bright-coloured flowers and herbs.

Praise and bless my Lord,
Thank Him and serve Him,
With all humility."

As soon as Francis became a little stronger, he was taken to Rieti where he lay in the palace in great pain. He missed the countryside, the music of the friars singing, the singing of the birds. He asked a brother who had a violin to play for him but Elias said that it was not proper music for a man near death who everybody knew was a holy saint. That night, as Francis lay awake and alone in the silence of the sleeping town, he was entertained by a violin being played as if an angel had come to earth.

Francis longed to return to his little cell at the Portiuncula but he was too famous to do what he wanted and doctors were brought to try and cure his eyes. The cure, which was more like a torture, consisted of burning the temples with hot tongs. His brother friars could not bear to watch and hurriedly left the room, but Francis waited calmly. When he felt the heat as the red-hot tongs approached his face, he said, 'Be courteous to me, Brother Fire, for I have always loved you.'

Neither this nor any other treatment improved Francis' sight nor his health in general and everyone began to believe he could not live for much longer. He was carried on a bier in a long procession, more as a king would be attended than a humble little friar, and taken back to his home town of Assisi. On the way he insisted on giving away his cloak to a beggar and the brothers scolded him because as fast as they found him a new cloak he gave it away. This was the third one they'd provided on this journey alone.

Yet another summer and another winter passed and Francis did not die, although his sufferings grew more and more acute. He felt sorry for those who must look after him and pressed his doctor to tell him when his release would come. 'Dear father,' said the doctor, 'you'll be well soon enough, with the grace of God.'

But Francis replied, 'I am not a cowardly cuckoo to be afraid of death. Besides I feel so close to God that I am equally content to live or die.' So the doctor told him the truth. He would not live beyond September or early October.

Francis smiled and said, 'Then welcome, Sister Death.'

At last he was allowed to leave Assisi and go back to the Portiuncula. The friars followed along, singing, at his request, the song he had made up, 'The Canticle of the Sun'. Once more Francis could delight in the fresh air on his skin and the warmth of the mellow autumn sun. Once more he could smell the scents of wild flowers, of the rosemary and thyme and hear the coo of the wood pigeons and the twitter of the smaller birds.

At a bend in the upward path where Francis knew the city would be visible, although he, of course, could no longer see it, he asked for the procession to stop and he raised his hands in blessing over the city where he was born.

The leaves were beginning to turn golden and swallows were gathering to fly away to warmer homes for the winter when he arrived back at his little cell.

One night Francis whispered to Brother Leo who was always near at hand, 'Write to Brother Giacoma and ask her to bring a pillow, candles, a tunic to lay me out in and a little of the frangipani marzipan.'

Just as he had finished speaking, there was a commotion at the door, stamping horses, jingling harness, loud voices, and in rushed Giacoma herself. Even more strangely, she had with her the very things that Francis had asked for. Crouching besides his bed, she explained that she had been praying when she had suddenly been certain that Francis needed her. She had mounted her horse at once and ridden with all speed from Rome.

Meanwhile Francis' other friend, Sister Clare, was also sick, although not near to death. Indeed she lived till she was an old woman. But Francis knew she would be unhappy not to see him before he died. So he called a brother to him, 'Go and tell Sister Clare to put aside her sorrow,' he whispered. 'Tell her that she will see me again and will be consoled.'

All the brothers gathered round Francis as his breath became weaker and he could no longer speak. They were still singing to him and reading from St. John's gospel when his spirit left his body.

It was twilight, a time of day when the night birds are beginning to haunt the woods and the cheerful birds of day have gone back to their nests. Suddenly the sky above Francis' cell was filled with a flock of larks, flying round and round and singing as joyfully as if the sun was just rising and a new day begun.

News of Francis' death spread quickly. That night he was allowed to lie quietly in St. Mary of the Angels. But the next morning a huge crowd came out from Assisi and the surrounding villages to escort his body to St. Georgio's Church where, as a child, he had gone to school. The crowd waved branches and flowers, played trumpets and beat drums so that it was more like a triumphant march than a funeral.

When they reached St. Damiano's, they stopped and Clare came to the window. She stretched her arms through the grill and touched Francis' hands. At once all her sadness at his death was gone and she felt a great surge of joy. So Francis' promise had become true.

Now there was nothing left to do but bury Francis' body. In his humility, he had wanted to be laid at the far end of town where criminals were executed.

At first nobody took any notice of his wish and only later his tomb was removed there and a magnificent cathedral built over it in his honour.

But Francis had never wanted grandeur and his spirit can be found more truly under a beech tree on the high slopes of Mount La Verna or in a cool cave on Mount Subasio or wherever a bird dips and dives above the tree-tops or the sun shines on a brightly coloured flower or where a poor man comes hopefully with hand outstretched.